Peony in Adoration

Reflections at the Feet of Jesus

by

Shannon Kurtz

AuthorHouse™
1663 Liberty Drive, Suite 200
Bloomington, IN 47403
www.authorhouse.com
Phone: 1-800-839-8640

First published by AuthorHouse   9/4/2007

ISBN: 978-1-4343-2583-9 (sc)
ISBN: 978-1-4343-2982-0 (hc)

Library of Congress Control Number: 2007905603

Printed in the United States of America
Bloomington, Indiana

This book is printed on acid-free paper.

All Scripture quotations taken from <u>*The New American Bible,*</u>
World Publishing, Inc. Grand Rapids, Michigan, Copyright © 1987.

"Rachel's Lament" was first published in St. Linus Review.
"Little Girl in the Choir Loft" was first published in Prairie Voices.

Dedication

For Glenn, who always believes in me.

Contents

Foreword

A truly gifted poet is one who is able to sculpt in words the sentiments, hopes, desires, aspirations, and prayers present within the human heart and give them expression, meaning, and direction. Shannon Kurtz is one such poet. Her poetry flows from her passion for truth, love of beauty, unbounded trust in God, and a sincere desire not only to be the best that she can, but to help her readers achieve their fullest human potential as well. I highly recommend this book to all who wish to go beyond the surface of life's experience and find their true worth hidden in the inner recesses of their own hearts where God dwells and which her book, *Peony in Adoration, Reflections at the Feet of Jesus*, will help to unlock.

Fr. John P. Grigus, O.F.M. Conv.
Spiritual Advisor,
Pope John Paul II Eucharistic Adoration Association of the Archdiocese of Chicago

Introduction

In December of 2001, I returned to the Catholic Church after twenty years as an Evangelical Protestant. During those years away, I grew to love Jesus Christ more deeply, especially through the study of His Word, the Holy Scriptures. It was my hunger for complete union with Him in the Holy Eucharist that brought me Home to the Catholic Church.

Adoration of Jesus in the Blessed Sacrament has become an important part of my life since my return. When I spend time with Jesus, my desire is to love and listen to Him the way Mary of Bethany did as she sat at His feet, when He visited her home. Just as surely as Jesus was there at Bethany, He is Truly Present to us and with us in Eucharistic Adoration. He loves us and is waiting for us to come. Then as we are together, He has things to tell each of us when we are quiet enough to listen.

When I wrote my first poem, "Like Mary of Bethany," the poetry surprised me. I had always enjoyed writing but had never written any serious poetry. Most of the reflections in this book flowed from thoughts or impressions that I had while in Adoration or at Mass. Sometimes a word or two, perhaps a phrase, would come to mind. A few of the poems came together almost at once, but most came to life after ruminating on a word or phrase for weeks or months.

There isn't anything we can't take to Jesus in Eucharistic Adoration: the people He has placed in our lives, our joys and sorrows, our wounded souls in need of healing. Spending time with Him brings with it a deeper awareness of His creation, His passion, His love, and His mercy for the whole world.

It is my hope that as you read these Scripture passages and "poem prayers," your own reflections will draw you ever closer to our Lord Jesus Christ and to His Blessed Mother, who is our mother as well.

His Creation

Some of the Pharisees in the crowd said to him, "Teacher, rebuke your disciples." He said in reply, "I tell you, if they keep silent, the stones will cry out!"

Luke 19:39-40

Peony in Adoration

Pure white petals raised in praise
Its fragrance potent praying,
Knows the purpose of its days.
It was made for this,
Can do no other
Than bloom, in love with its Creator!
Humbled by this faithful flower's
Total love, enthralled and glory telling,
For I have turned to other suns
Drew nourishment not filling.
A messenger, this Peony, heralding the way
Speaks above stony silence
As I go about my day.

Advent

Naked oak shivers

Awaiting snowy vestments,

Lace embroidery.

January Sunset

Marbleized molten
Creamsicle sky
Volcano of color
Stuns the eye.
Inhaling snow sparkles
Fresh blossoms hid
Leaping heart longs
For New Life ahead.

Awakening

May breezes rustle
Lily of the valley bed
Ringing tiny bells.

Sunlit Adoration

The sun shines on the Son of God
Play of light on the Light of the World.
Birds chirp praise to their Maestro
The gentle breeze, a ballet.
Love feast's mute observer
I sit.
Unable to illumine You as the sun or
Serenade You as the birds of the air,
Caress You as the wind.
Still You think of me—
Oh that my silence could give You such praise!

Where Do the Leaves Go?

Where do the leaves go
After they fall,
When wind blows the reds,
The oranges, the golds, and all?

Back to their Maker
The God of all gods
To pave heaven's walkway
His wounded feet trod.

His Character

In the beginning was the Word, and the Word was with God, and the Word was God.

John 1:1

The Word

No tongue can tell
For in each word
The Word's character dwells.
For in each word as
Each word was conceived,
Is Man's inept description
Of what is received.

The Big Lie

For every evil,

There is the big why:

God doesn't care,

The devil's big lie.

Yes, there's a God, but He doesn't love you

He will not reply.

Don't you know it's useless?

He's deaf to your cries.

Yet when your prayers are so deep

They come forth as sighs

Your tears touch Me deeply,

I do more than stand by.

How imperceptible My workings

This, My reply:

Hang on, I AM not helpless

This situation, not yours to know why

Trust Me, I love you

I cannot lie.

His Blessed Mother

Mary said, "Behold, I am the handmaid of the Lord. May it be done to me according to your word."

Luke 1:38

Fiat

She heard You call
By messenger
This Mary, Handmaid of the Lord
Still loving You, accepted
The relationship that led to the Child.
Let it be done,
Your Word—the
Seed of New Life
Unto me.
Into an ancient garden,
The Root of Jesse
Planted in soil long prepared
Blossomed not just the flower,
But flowering Life
Lily of the Valley,
The Rose of Sharon.
Bright and Morning Star
Arose, when time was full,
Decaying, overripe.
She brought forth her only Son
With love she tucked
The Lamb of God
Into hallowed hay,
Shepherds as sentinels
To keep the wolves away.

Mary of Seasons

Mary, as you pondered,
Was your soul in Winter
At the manger, in the Temple,
In Egypt, among strangers,
As you waited, watched in the hidden
Wondered at His
Graceful stature and wisdom.

Mary, as you pondered,
Was your soul in Springtime
As no longer silent,
His new Life blossomed,
Up from thawing still waters
Full jugs, perfect New Wine.

Mary, as you pondered,
Was your soul in Summer
As light days were longer
He fed from bounty, teaching,
Releasing torment and fear.
Soil tilled in compassion
Considered the lilies, healing,
Revealing, making holy.

Mary, as you pondered,
Was your soul in Autumn
When harvest came, ready
On high place, all captives freed—
Shared your perfect Lamb as oblation
So we could partake,
Of your Fruit plucked from the Tree.

Mary, as you pondered,
Was your soul in Winter
In the Finished,
The grave cloths
Swaddling Sacrifice,
Caressing His Head.

Then! Was your pondering sweet,
Tomb empty, were you first to see
After three days, embracing
New Life, New Spring!

Oh, Mary of Seasons,
Waiting, the watching
The Silence, the end.
Of birthing and new life
And hope for all men.
In you we see help
In all our ponderings,
In all our whens.

Happy Birthday, Mother

Happy birthday, Mother
Too many spent away
Not knowing your love
Drew me, longing for the Taste.

Happy birthday, Mother
In the shadow of the Son
Points to closer kinship
With the Holy One.

Happy Birthday, Mother
So many years ignored
Did not change your heart
For me, love outpoured.

Happy birthday, Mother
For this child motherless
Holy maiden warrior
Never left the watch.

Happy birthday, Mother
All He tells me do
Is holy completion
Leading Home to you.

Happy birthday, Mother
I have come to say
Though decades gone, I love you
I am Home to stay.

"And how does this happen to me, that the mother of my Lord should come to me? For at the moment the sound of your greeting reached my ears, the infant in my womb leaped for joy."

Luke 1:43-44

Behold the Lamb of God

In womb's darkness
Before I saw the sun,
Danced I before Him
As David once had done
Impossible met Incarnate
When my soul beheld the Son.

My mother hailed the Mother of
One Word spoken, in the Ark of grace.
My father's silence begat
The lone voice crying,
Make straight the paths before Him
Behold the Lamb of God.

His Gospel

As they continued their journey he entered a village where a woman whose name was Martha welcomed him. She had a sister named Mary who sat beside the Lord at his feet listening to him speak. Martha, burdened with much serving, came to him and said, "Lord, do you not care that my sister has left me by myself to do the serving? Tell her to help me." The Lord said to her in reply, "Martha, Martha, you are anxious and worried about many things. There is need of only one thing. Mary has chosen the better part and it will not be taken from her."

Luke 10:38-42

Like Mary of Bethany

Precious Jesus, Presence True
Humbly sitting at Your feet
I come today incomplete.
Like Mary, oh deprive me not
Of finer things, portion, lot.

Oh Needful Thing, my need fulfill
Of finer things, better part.
Feed the hunger in my heart—
With Bread, Your Holy Presence Real
Which none can take away or steal.

Sweet Jesus in Holy Mystery,
Gather in Your loving arms
This Mary after Your own heart.
Oh Giver of the finer things,
My dearest, dearest Better Part.

Martha

But today like Mary I am not,
Martha sits in Mary's spot.
Needing gratitude
A longing that is not new,
For all the burdened serving I must do.

But, ah, that's it, Lord, the crux of it—
The more I need, demand my due
I rush and wander far
From You, my Guest,
The finest Thing, the Better Part.

My Messiah, God's own Son
Whatever of Him You ask He'll do.
So ask Him, Lord, that as I serve
Make me after Your own heart,
My dearest, dearest Better Part.

*When it was evening, he reclined at table with
the Twelve. And while they were eating, he said,
"Amen, I say to you, one of you will betray me."
Deeply distressed at this, they began to say to him
one after another, "Surely it is not I, Lord?"*

Matthew 26:20-22

Surely It Is I, Lord

Surely it is I, Lord,
One who eats Your Body
Drinks Your Precious Blood
While many are freezing,
Rubbing my gloved hands
Over affluence bonfire.
Blind to naked, strewn body parts
Arrogantly selfish—not rending my garments of heart.
Detouring around homeless and dying,
The much easier way.
In withholding a cup of cold water
From thirsting
Not willing to drink of Your Cup.
How like Peter I am
You know that I love You!
Seventy times seven my heart pleas:
Please! Restore to me sight to see
As Your heart sees and
Your love for Your least of these.

"And the king will say to them in reply, 'Amen, I say to you, whatever you did for one of these least brothers of mine, you did for me.'"

Matthew 25:40

The Door Knocks

The Door knocks,
You've been in there too long
It's time to come out and hear the world's song:
Feed me,
I need,
Please
To be freed
Begging cacophony sung by throngs.
Contemplation needs action
Meeting needs in the doing
Calls me back to my knees
Till outside the Door knocks,
You've been in there too long.
It's time to come out and hear the world's song.

"So do not be afraid; you are worth more than many sparrows."

Matthew 10:31

Trust

In a clap of spring thunder
Sparrow sings
As trust wings.
But I, being worth far more,
Fear to trust
As storm brings
The very thing
That makes me need You the most.
Oh Great Mystery!

"Come to me, all you who labor and are burdened, and I will give you rest. Take my yoke upon you and learn from me, for I am meek and humble of heart; and you will find rest for yourselves. For my yoke is easy, and my burden is light."

Matthew 11:28-30

Perfect Yoke

My smooth wooden yoke, its perfect fit chafing;
Against One shouldering, I fight.
Unjust, unfair this yoke I'm pressed to wear!
But there was a creature with shoulders relaxed
Peaceful, content, seemingly free.

Intrigued, I surveyed his countenance calm
In perfectly shaped yoke shouldered by Might
Serenity bore burdens hidden from sight.
His smooth wooden yoke, a mantle bestowed
In glint of sunlight I beheld burnished gold.

He said, "To what shall we compare the kingdom of God?... It is like a mustard seed that, when it is sown in the ground, is the smallest of all the seeds of the earth. But once it is sown, it springs up and becomes the largest of plants and puts forth large branches, so that the birds of the sky can dwell in its shade."

Mark 4:30-32

Mustard Seed

Lord, I would be Your mustard seed
My spirit's soil please till,
To be and do and grow for You
Plant me where You will.

Lord, let me be Your mustard seed
Smallest of them all,
Hide me in Your soil of love
To be and grow and live.

Lord, pour faith into this mustard seed
To grow in quiet whisper of Your grace,
Let Your Spirit stir the branches
That long to stroke Your Face.

When Jesus was born in Bethlehem of Judea, in the days of King Herod, behold, magi from the east arrived in Jerusalem, saying, "Where is the newborn king of the Jews? We saw his star at its rising and have come to do him homage."

Matthew 2:1-2

Airport Christmas

Great undulating desert
Asphalt mirage, no heat.
Great migrating birds
Just touching down
No resting, no nest.
Disembarked throngs
March past counterfeit trees.
Silver tinsel garland obscures
Bright shining star
In the East,
Traveling, traveling
Finding no peace.

"But whoever drinks the water I shall give will never thirst; the water I shall give will become in him a spring of water welling up to eternal life."

John 4:14

Living Water

For so long I have pondered the living water symbolism and substance. I have taken note of the many references to water in Your Word, and I love the fact that my name, Shannon, is also the name of a river.

I long to be filled with Your living water; may I be a river in more than name only. Overflow the banks of my spirit with Your Holy Spirit—living water.

When my river freezes over, blow Your thawing wind to melt its hardened surface.

When my river is choppy and storm-filled, calm its waves with Your gentle hand and quieting Word.

When I am thirsty and parched and don't realize that I am, lead me to drink deeply of Your refreshment.

When I am floating, buoyant in Your care, may the joy and mystery of those moments sustain me in the storm.

When I am stagnant, easily offended and myopic, blow a misty cloud of Your dew over my horizon to water and fill this river as the rains water the River Shannon.

May Your rain on this river make my soul a rich and verdant resting place for You, my Jesus, in Your Eucharistic, Powerful Presence.

Amen.

And He asked them, "But who do you say that I am?"

Mark 8:29

Who Do You Say That I Am?

I say You are my savior, my love, my healer, my joy, my all in all.

You are the poetry in my soul.

You are my funny friend.

You are the yellow, gold, orange, and red of autumn.

You are my shining sun and my bright moon.

You are the reason I live.

In You I move and live and have my being.

You are the God of widows and orphans.

You are my comfort.

You are my food in the Holy Eucharist.

You are forgiveness.

You are the music I sing.

You are the director of this play, which is my life, acted out in this place where I live.

In the final scene, may I be escorted off-stage by the angels, into Your waiting arms.

Amen

He said to them, "When you pray, say: Father, hallowed be your name, your kingdom come. Give us each day our daily bread and forgive us our sins for we ourselves forgive everyone in debt to us..."

Luke 11:2-4

My Toolbox

I have a toolbox. It was given to me on the day I was born. However, I didn't find it listed in my baby book along the other gifts like the yellow receiving blanket from Aunt Thelma or the teething ring from Grandma. I can't see it or touch it. I can't pick out the tools that I think I'd like to have. In fact, I can't get the toolbox open. Only the Giver of this special box knows the contents and when I will need to use a tool.

At times, my toolbox seemed too heavy to carry. It was during one of those times that the Giver came along beside me. It was time for Him to open the box. I knelt down close to Him as He showed me all He had prepared for my use. My toolbox is constructed of steel. It's strong and sturdy with limitless size. There is room for every kind of tool He knows I will ever need.

The first tools He showed me were my parents. "They were the specially selected tools I used to give you life," the Giver said. The next tool was a reciprocating saw. It was the grief I had endured since their deaths. It cut to the deepest part of my soul, yet I could not grieve if I did not love. That grief was a tool I could use to comfort others.

Disguised as screwdrivers of various sizes, humor was lurking in several of the little compartments of my toolbox ready to pop out at just the right moment. I was to use humor in the situations when the nuts and bolts of life were screwed in too tightly.

Next I found a measuring tape. It was just my size. I was not to measure myself against others. I was to use it as a guide to what I was measuring up to be. "Much has been given to you," the Giver said. "Much will be required."

As I continued to look through my toolbox I found a level. If I set my life on shifting ground, things would get cock-eyed and off balance. Instead,

His level would guide me in straight paths. "At times I will ask you to lend this level to others," the Giver said, "especially to your children, to help them make sense of life's vertigo."

The Giver continued showing me the tools. There was a large compartment that was empty except for a tiny speck of rust in the middle of it. "That tool is humility," the Giver said. "It will grow and become truly beautiful the more you step back so others can go forward."

I found a wrench, a vise, and a metal file. As I picked up each one, they felt familiar to me, like old friends. "Yes, you do recognize them," the Giver said. "They are molding and shaping you into the person I made you to be."

Then I saw an oil can, but when I picked it up, the label read *Tears*. It was only half full. "I have saved every tear you have ever cried," He said. "They are the lubricant for your life's experiences. There are still many more to be shed."

Next I found a hammer, but just one nail. "The nail is Faith. It has been set into a Sure Place since you were a little girl and first used this hammer of prayer." And I was ashamed of the times I laid down my hammer when I knew the nail had come loose. "Each person has a toolbox," the Giver said. "When you laid down your hammer, when you were too frightened, too worried, or too weak to use it, I had others pick up their hammers in your stead."

My toolbox still seemed too heavy, I was sure I couldn't go on. "Some of the tools in your toolbox were always meant to be shared. It has become heavy with bits of things broken and a tool you are hoarding."

This time He placed something into my hand. It was a bottle of wood glue labeled *Forgiveness*. The cap was stuck on, the label was smudged, the contents dried up. "Just one drop from this bottle will lighten your load and make room for other tools your toolbox should hold."

I began to squeeze the bottle, and to my surprise as I kept squeezing, the glue became a soft, flowing liquid. With my other hand I held a broken framed picture that had been hidden under some debris in my toolbox. As my hand shook, I dabbed some of the glue into the crack in the picture frame. Then I let the glue flow, filling all the little crevices in the crack. My heart became lighter as I looked at the face in the picture frame smiling back at me. Lovingly I placed the photograph back into my toolbox. "Stand up now and pick up your toolbox," the Giver said. "Its weight will be perfect." And so it was.

His Passion

But he was pierced for our offenses, crushed for our sins, upon him was the chastisement that makes us whole, by his stripes we were healed.

Isaiah 53:5

Thorns

Thorns in toil the Father sent
And cursed the soil you'll work,
As all to disobey are bent.

His Son to Earth the Father sent,
Though cursed, unworthy those He loved
For all of history, the Event.

A crown of thorns for mockery meant
Was laid upon that Holy Head.
From curséd ground no longer choked,
A laurel wreath as
It is finished, He spoke.

Thorns some days my Savior sends
As splinters, somehow as friends
To keep me close, trust Him. Be.
Reminder of those
He wore for me.

"Daughters of Jerusalem, do not weep for me; weep instead for yourselves and for your children..."

Luke 23:28

Rachel's Lament

Watching You struggle and stumble the Way
The shouting and chaos brings back a day filled with promise
Turned monstrously black, when Herod's death squad stopped,
Did not Passover.
Ragged sobs escape from deep within—
Seeing You, I wonder
If he had lived, what would my Innocent be?
How is it You live today
And why did You escape Herod's decree?
If my son had lived, he would be thirty and three.
In You the man I imagine I see—
The man my son may have been.
I weep not just for You, I'm weeping for me.
How could I know Your mother wept too?
That because my son died
You could live to die too?
Oh, dear Rachel, your lament has been heard.
I see in your soul the grief that you bear
In giving your son, behold your redemption is near.

Crimson Neon

Jesus, what flashed through Your mind
Just at the moment before—for all these You died
Who for ages and eons
On our knees would not kneel on
To worship or lean on,
Arguing, fighting about what to agree on
Alas, it's all about me on
This earth You created.

Co-opted by corruption, collusion, conflict,
Coveting, craving, cunning,
Conviction, consternation, craftiness chronic,
Carousing, confusion, criminal carnage.
Your Cross coalesced
In conquering death
For all ages and eons
Writ crimson neon.

His Eucharistic Presence

He said to Peter, "Simon, are you asleep? Could you not keep watch for one hour?"

Mark 14:37

Making a Visit

Pulling the heavy door with all my might,
Looking in— to see His red lamp burning.
Then tiptoeing up the Mary side aisle,
Dropped my nickel, clink in the slot.
I lit a candle full of childish prayers
He heard because He was waiting there.
Then our visits ended,
I went my way.

In my twenty years away from the Fold,
Our visits long distance, in Letters of old.
Read, re-read, memorized, treasured,
Close to my heart, loving Him more
As His Word came alive, drawing me, calling me.
I heard because He was waiting there.
Then I made a visit,
I came Home to stay.

At Your Feet

Jesus, I know You are here

Just as I know what is real around me.

So often stirred—and propelled—

To put on paper what cannot be understood.

It seems right somehow to be sitting

At Your feet.

How You have waited, watching

While I pleased myself,

Not pleasing You.

Security Blanket

I touched the hem
Of Your garment today.
Your power touched me,
You looked my way.

Your hem's satiny fabric
Caressed my cheek,
Security, Comfort.
I am so weak.

Tip of My Tongue

It seems rather redundant to be journaling my thoughts, my dreams, my frustrations, and my prayers while seated before You, Yourself, Truly Present under the appearance of Bread in the Monstrance. You already know about everything, but You want me to share it all with You. When I pray or write or cry out to you, Lord, it's from the point of being needy in the area of language. Just like the English as a second language students I tutor, who struggle for just the right word to convey what they mean, I struggle to give voice to words that are in a language that I will never know until I am with You in Heaven. But Jesus, accept my pitiful moanings, utterings, and grammar gaffes. How in this world could I possibly tell You how much I love You?

For so long I was frustrated, as if every moment I lived as one with something on the tip of my tongue—that couldn't be spoken no matter how hard I tried. That frustration melted away the first time I received You in Holy Eucharist after my return to the Church after so many years away. The perfect Word I had been searching for was You. On my tongue, so incapable of expression came the Word made flesh, the Creator of that very tongue. I am awestruck at how this comes to be, the richness of it all. You, who are the be all and end all, encapsulate all things and in You all things on Earth and in Heaven hold together.

Even in this bliss, dear Jesus, the cares and fears of my life jump up and down, waving their arms like preschool students, waiting to be called on by the teacher. How I wish I could ignore them, but instead please accept them all as a bouquet of my love.

*Inspired by "Adoro Te Devote" by St. Thomas Aquinas and
its English translation by Gerard Manley Hopkins.*

My Adoro Te

Jesus, I am here now,
Sitting at Your feet
May my tears be incense,
Pleasing fragrance sweet.
Pouring out my heart to You
Because of all Thou art,
Promised Answer to the knock
On Your holy Heart.

Ashamed I might come asking,
But for Your saving grace
Gives me courage, longing,
To look upon Your Face.
I see the Royal wounded Head,
Let me wipe your brow,
Once despised, rejected,
All comeliness is now.

Jesus, who art Lord of all,
Yet all You set aside,
Making Yourself nothing,
Humbled for the pride.
Took our very nature
When on the Cross You died,
To be exalted in heaven and earth
By Your ransomed bride.

Behind the Veil the ancients
Knew the Presence dwelt.
Awestruck at Your Power
Priest in holy belt,
Until the perfect Sacrifice
The veil split in two,
Awestruck to be kneeling here,
Before Your Presence True.

Until then, my Lord Jesus,
As I run my race,
Contented in Your Presence
Here in this holy place,
Knowing that You wait for me
As I await the Taste,
Until in heaven, Jesus,
I see You Face to face.

Sacred Hearth

Under my roof unworthy
Awaiting Your approach,
Begging: Cross the threshold,
Come unto my hearth.
Unshod, I wait on tiptoe
As Essence enters in.
One Word transforms this hovel
Into holy ground again.

Sweet Communion

In perfect sweet communion
Comes together death and life.
Eating the Body, drinking the Blood shed
Until not one ounce was left,
By His atoning, not bereft.
To understand not my privilege,
Belief I must voice
That Jesus loves me
Saved me by choice,
To carry His Life in my body
To life in the Body of Christ.

Traveling Blessings

I come here today

For traveling blessings

On circuitous route,

Heading north via westward that on arrival

Bringing You-ness to each that I meet.

Telling the hope that is in me

To each that I greet,

Knowing You walk

Before me and as I take a seat.

Be blessed for the Good News on

My wandering feet.

Tending those who so love You

But hungry, needing

Your Body to eat.

May my words be comfort, not confusing,

As Your Spirit whispers

Silence! or Speak.

His Servants

"His master said to him, 'Well done, my good and faithful servant. Since you were faithful in small matters, I will give you great responsibilities. Come, share your master's joy.' "

Matthew 25:21

The Keys

We kept watch in the courtyard
Under the window as prayers in foreign accents
Were said for the man dying up there.
The Keys were not missing,
Just set aside, as with his last breath
He stretched out his hands,
Releasing the Keys in trade for his prize.

In a temple courtyard
Near a smoky bonfire, warming
The first keeper, being sifted like wheat,
Threw down the Keys in defeat
As he heard the cock crow in mourning greet.

At the seashore's charcoal fire
When the smoke cleared, this man was restored
He again held the Keys, returned by his Lord.
The coward became courage fluently speaking
The Truth in all languages
Spoken in known world seeking.

His successive keepers
For twenty centuries have held
Some binding tightly, some often too loose
By ring fingers kissed,
But the Owner promised forever
To keep His Keys from the abyss.

In the square watching the window,
Eyes hungry to see
By picking them up, who the new keeper will be.
Ambiguous smoke clearing to white
Bells ring out *Benedictus!*
Humbly picks up the Keys.

*For Fr. Robert C. Dressman, S.J. on the occasion of the
fiftieth anniversary of his ordination to the Priesthood*

In Persona Christi

The grace of a glimpse

Allowed me to see

An eternal moment

Not hidden from Thee.

In a chapel for twelve

Stood the priest, tall,

Un-stooped with age,

Presiding that day

As for a half century,

Daily, each sacrifice new.

A crucifix hanging

Behind the altar, as

His arms outstretched

Orans perfectly mirrored the template

Of the Corpus hung there.

In Persona Christi

Anointed forever, Your priest

In Melchisedech's Order,

At each Consecration

Consecrating all that he is.

Holy Priest

The journey is too much
As beaten, weary boned
To the rear guard, trust Me—
I send. You are not alone.

You have been the raven
Water for parched souls,
I want you close beside Me
To heal prophetic toll.

In My power you saw, not as man sees
Reading precious souls I sent,
With your heart you heard them
In Persona Christi to those I lent.

The souls you shaped and
Carved and polished here are but just a few of
Jewels that someday will adorn
The Priestly crown prepared for you.

Ruthie

Lord, we see how much You loved her,
Raised her to new life
After all she served
Through sorrow's time
And happiness of life.
With undivided faith,
In readiness her lamp oiled
You whisked her to the Banquet Room
Your guest forever,
Her seat eternally prepared.
Now Lord, see how much we loved her,
Dumbfounded in our grief
We cry and laugh
And thank You for lending us
Our Village Martha.
She served You when serving us,
With her Mary heart.

I See Jesus

I thank my God upon every remembrance of you,

    For in you, I see Jesus.

        The One you love

        In Whom you live

        And breathe

    In you, I see Jesus.

        The One you preach

        And represent

        His attributes

    In you, I see Jesus.

        Displaying purity and loveliness

        Excellence of grace permeating

        Each act, each prayer, think on this

    In you, I see Jesus.

        When difficult the days you live

        With joy, enduring

        Holding fast, forgetting things behind

    In you, I see Jesus.

        Who is your strength

        More than worldly might,

        Trusting, as you live thus

    In you, I see Jesus.

        Considering yourself least

        Unselfish, not presuming

    Accepting your path, Humility

In you, I see Jesus.

    As directing my gaze

    My tongue must praise

    This One you love, your life displays

In you, I see Jesus.

I thank my God upon every remembrance of you,

For in you, I see Jesus.

His Healing

The LORD is close to the brokenhearted, saves those whose spirit is crushed.

Psalm 34:19

The Healing Box

Stepping in, the dim light hurts my eyes.

My knees bending, never low enough.

In halting speech, each syllable lifts weight

The patient Knife excising sin at its core,

Mercy lovingly accepts my tears drenching His Feet.

Forgiven— the sinful woman who entered,

Absolved— goes in peace, His little child.

Mother Loss

Again I struggle and have to wonder
Why often it seems the good die so young,
Mothers are left with lives torn asunder.

Again I ask God, why such a blunder?
Too many homes where black bunting is hung,
I cry and pray and struggle and wonder.

Why a mother's left, life torn asunder
Hopes, dreams, memories, eternity flung,
The phone call of news, a clap of thunder.

The mother cries, prays, struggles, and wonders:
Could she from this life also be sprung,
To escape from her life torn asunder?

Bearing grief's armor, too numb to ponder,
Her screams not escaping her useless lungs
For one whom she carried, once part of her.

This wonder of life, her work of splendor
Touched so many lives while still so young.
Her treasured child, this gift that God lent her
In death always with her, that is the wonder.

Love-Struck

A love-struck maiden, you,
Bedecked in mountaintop tulle
Promised to follow Me. No matter.
Happy, giddy, your radiant form
Unprepared for Union's first storm.
Romantic gondola ride you imagined
Left you rocked, propelled into the sea.
Flimsy faith floated, bobbed, strangled, despair.
You could not know when we wed
Numberless ways you'd be dismayed, disobey,
Break promises made.
Each time rescued, see in rearview
Your first love untried, but never untrue.

My Peace Is Pain

Peace I leave with you
Not as the world gives, I.
In receiving My Peace,
Self has to die.

Peace I leave with you
Not as the world gives, I.
In accepting My Peace,
I give you My Pain.

His Gift of Faith

Lord, you have been our refuge through all generations.

Psalm 90:1

Faith of My Mothers

To Ireland's Rock of Cashel I came as a pilgrim that day
The high holy place of Druid, Celt, and Saint Patrick some say.
Stepping into the vestige of antiquity's hush
On a forsaken altar, I eternity touched.
Centuries connected in Faith succession,
I stood in the midst of a living Faith lesson
For after years of singing the hymn, I knew
The "Faith of Our Fathers" lyrics were true.

Then I stepped out through an archway
Into soft splattered sunshine, and saw to the west
A rainbow end at Kilfeakle, where some of my people rest.
But I knew that in my family, at least,
It was the women who had lived and passed on that Faith best.

So as loved ones around them died in hunger and shame,
First Catherine, then Mary, left Ireland whispering Your Name.
Farther west than Connaught,
To a new land they journeyed,
From Tipperary, clutching bundles
Empty but for the Faith they carried.

With its comfort and strength, they continued to live
And to model, giving voice and expression to
The quieter Faith of their husbands, brothers, and fathers.

Then I recalled it was three years to the day
You welcomed me Home
To the Faith of my mothers to stay,
The Faith they followed up to their last days.
And in that moment You showed me,
As I peeked over Your shoulder
The scrapbook You keep of Your sons and daughters.
Then pointing Your finger to my mothers in Faith,
Showed the resemblance I bear to my Mother,
Grandmothers, Aunt Helen, Aunt Kate.
Oh such a Gift! This Faith
My mothers passed on to me.
May I live it well till the end of my days,
Passing it on to those who follow me.

Angel of God

In the dormer bedroom
I knelt by her side.
"Repeat after me,
Angel of God, my Guardian dear
It's not hard to say."
So with those words,
She taught me to pray.

Dusky bedtime, August heat
To whom God's love commits me here
Hands folded like hers
With her faraway gaze,
She was back with her mother
Who taught her to pray.

Then leaning close, she whispered,
"Because God is kind
He gave you an angel to *rule and guard*
To ever this day be at your side
Into God's light your constant guide."

On that first night of many,
Angel of God, my Guardian dear,
Repeating those words,
As I knelt beside her
It's not hard to say,
I first learned God loved me
When she taught me to pray.

The Bells of Saint Boniface

I can remember a much simpler day
When tolling bells told the end of our play.

The bells that were tolled told time and routine
Time to go out and time to come in.

The bells that were tolled each morning at eight
If not in the classroom, meant we were late.

The bells that were tolled before daily Mass
As we processed in—in order by class.

The bells that were tolled as we followed sad
Too early Mom's casket, then too soon, our Dad's.

The bells were the pitch pipe of my life back then,
When they were tolled, I knew who I was
And where I had been.

On the day of my wedding, in the stairway
Next to their ropes I was hid
A bride, a woman, no longer a kid.

Then I thought back remembering a much simpler day,
When the bells of Saint Boniface marked out our days.

Bridal Shop Time Machine

Stepping into the bridal shop time machine

I see a young woman engaged to be married

Who just wore a christening gown,

Rode a stroller, tricycle, Schwinn, drove Mercury Cougar.

Our special date to go shopping when she was four, at

Tyson's Corner, Hello Kitty Store.

Rainbow Bright bedroom, Strawberry Shortcake nightgown

Preschool fieldtrip to a farm, silo brimming with corn.

Remembering her pulling the string of Mattel See and Say.

What does the cow say? Moo. What does the pig say? Oink.

Playing with Fisher-Price farm animals on the kitchen floor.

Hot lunch today or sack lunch with milk money?

Giggling slumberless parties, many good friends.

Piano lessons, practices, and recitals

For life's recitals, practices, and lessons.

Missing teeth tree rings.

Sometimes a teasing big sister, but cared for her brother

With cool washcloth on his fevered brow

Because that's what Auntie Em did for Dorothy.

In three flower-girl dresses, one each white, pink, and peach,

Down church middle aisles, walking just so.

Of practical jokes, romance, and gossip made privy

While minivan chauffeuring, not really eavesdropping.

Prom dresses, accessories, hairdos, corsages,

Trombone lessons, marching, symphonic, and jazz bands first chair.

First day of school, then moving to college

Four hours away, on her own.

Now she's fallen in love

This one's a keeper.

I review life's drive-thru window moments

And wish I'd gone inside and made them last longer.

The way-back machine drops me off just in time,

To see my child, who just wore a christening gown,

Wearing the wedding dress of her dreams.

Little Girl in the Choir Loft

As most of my Dad's contemporaries were on the downward side of parenting, he was just beginning that adventure. With my birth, my Dad became a father for the first time when he was forty-two. Within ten years, there were six of us kids. Sometimes I wondered if he ever really knew what hit him, like the time he decided that using Robert's Rules of Order might be a good way to control the conversation at the dinner table.

The first evening, we kids thought it was great fun. If one of us wished to speak, we were to raise our hand to request permission to speak. The Chair, being Dad, would recognize us and then we could talk. Things went very smoothly the first evening. As soon as we had finished saying grace the next evening, my brother requested permission to speak. When Dad gave him permission, he yelled, "Speak, speak, speak!" Then the rest of us joined the chant and it all went downhill from there. We returned to our former topics, such as knock-knock and elephant jokes.

I was crazy about my Dad. He valued and accepted me, and not just because I was his child. He treated me with respect. He never made me feel that I was annoying or behaving in a childlike manner. He must have sensed a kindred-ness, a thinker part of me that was so like him. He nurtured that. Sometimes in the evening he and I would sit together at the kitchen table. I would be doing my homework, he would be reading a detective novel. We discussed baseball and bombs, card games and communism, poetry and politics. He taught and I caught. Dad could be aloof at times, keeping much of his life close to the vest. He drank. He was a musician. He worked hard. He struggled.

Some of my favorite times with my Dad were in the church choir loft when he sang for a wedding. I loved the fancy dresses, the romance, the "Ave Maria." He was in great demand as a soloist. He would sometimes have to sight-read a piece of music for the first time before Mass, and then he would sing it as though it was a standard in his repertoire. I loved the Irish tenor side of him. I was proud to be seen with him, to be his daughter.

When it was time for Communion, I walked down from the choir loft to receive Holy Eucharist. My Dad never did. Looking back now, I realize there may have been some good reasons, not the least of which was that he was being paid to sing, usually "Panis Angelicus," during Communion. But for a little girl like me, that would not do. How could he not receive Jesus in Holy Communion?

Each Sunday he was the paid soloist for noon Mass at a local parish. Since he was usually out till the early hours of the morning singing and playing trombone in a dance band, this fit his schedule well. I often attended that Mass with him. He didn't receive the Holy Eucharist on Sundays either. I longed to see him perform the Catholic rituals.

But my Dad had a spiritual side. There are two instances I remember vividly. When I dramatically pronounced my adoration for a new brand of pineapple juice, he corrected not only my grammar but also my theology by staunchly defending the definition of the word *adore*. "You may like that juice," he replied, "but you may only adore God." My sense of wonder at that exchange has never left me.

During one of our kitchen table talks, when I was about ten years old, I asked him if he thought God ever laughed. Dad sat back with a dreamy gleam in his eye. He began to grin, and chuckling, he said, "I'm sure God looks down from heaven and gets His jollies." The tenderness of that moment was a gift to me, from my earthly Dad and my Heavenly Father.

His drinking began to spiral out of control when Mom died of cancer, leaving him with six children under sixteen. Thankfully he entered treatment two years later and maintained his sobriety until his death. He told me sometime later that if he hadn't had us to care for and care about, he would have been dead within a few months as a result of his drinking. His spiritual side remained private. He rarely attended Mass those last few years.

After I left home, his health deteriorated as a result of his forty plus years of smoking. He was dying of emphysema. There were three hospitalizations when it was predicted he would not survive. Each time he rallied. In those last few months of his life, I feared for his soul. How long would he be angry with God? How long would God "wait" for him? I wanted Dad to be at peace in his final days here on Earth and to go to heaven when he died. I prayed, I cried, I begged God for a sign, something I could cling to so I could know my Dad was okay. I dreaded the thought of my Dad going to hell.

My husband and I had planned a trip to visit Navy friends in Europe. I was torn about whether to cancel the trip, but my brother reassured me that Dad was stable. Even better, he seemed to be truly at peace for the first time that anyone could remember. We left on our trip.

We arrived at our first stop, Shannon, Ireland. Jetlagged, we went directly to the airport hotel to sleep. I had a dream about Dad. He was wearing his green terry-cloth bathrobe, but it was brand new, not shabby and worn-out as before. He was standing on a stage with red velvety curtains opened wide. Then as I watched, two angelic beings approached him, one on either side. They gently escorted Dad offstage. I felt such peace. I knew Dad had died. I knew he was going to heaven. I knew we kids would be okay. I woke up and looked at the clock. It was 12:23 p.m. in Ireland. Comforted and peaceful, I went back to sleep.

An hour later I was awakened by the telephone. I picked it up, already knowing it would be my brother and what he would tell me. Dad had died in Michigan at 6:23 a.m., the exact time of my dream. God had told me. He had showed me and consoled me. He had bestowed on the little girl in the choir loft her heart's desire. Her Daddy was in heaven.

It has been nearly thirty years since Dad died. The dream is still fresh in my memory. The comforting thoughts as I awoke from that dream were promises God kept. He did watch over all of us. Even though we were orphans, He did not leave us or forsake us. There was pain. There were problems. But there was prayer and power and protection.

Now, when I picture Dad in heaven, he still wears the new green bathrobe. He is smiling, with his arm around Mom. Behold the old has become new. He is Home.

My Jesus Dear

Oh, how You wooed me, my Jesus dear

Come closer, come closer, come with no fear.

Oh, how You drew me, my Jesus dear

With trusting, with trusting, I've seen your tears.

Oh, how You pursued me, my Jesus dear

Your longing's My Longing, I'm always here.

Oh, how You led me, my Jesus dear

Waiting and watching, hoping you would appear.

Oh, how You prodded me, Jesus, my dear

Loving you, loving you, year after year.

Oh, how You fed me, Jesus, my dear

Your hunger, your hunger, I am Satisfier.

Oh, How You wooed me, Jesus so dear

I proclaim to the world,

"Lord, it's good to be here!"

To the one who is able to keep you from stumbling and to present you unblemished and exultant, in the presence of his glory, to the only God, our savior, through Jesus Christ our Lord be glory, majesty, power, and authority from ages past, now, and for ages to come. Amen

Jude 1:24-25

Acknowledgements

With deepest gratitude to my husband Glenn, my daughter Kelly,
my son-in-law Anthony, and my son Robert, for their constant love,
encouragement, and support.

For my parents, Peg and Jim Kelly, my sister Bridget, my brothers Matt,
Tim, Bob, and Terry. I am so thankful that God saw fit to make us a
family.

Thanks to Fr. Robert C. Dressman, S.J., Fr. Thomas L. Meagher, and
Fr. John P. Grigus, O.F.M. Conv., for their spiritual direction and for
nudging the writer in me.

With gratitude to Kelly Briggman, Maureen Stroia, Susan Tourtelot,
Janet Brakel, and Fr. Anthony Fox, O.F.M. Conv., for their suggestions,
proofreading, and editing help along the way.

To all the friars, staff, and volunteers at Marytown in Libertyville,
Illinois—thank you for Perpetual Adoration in Our Lady of the Blessed
Sacrament Chapel and for a quiet room in the retreat center, where much
of this book came together.

To all those who have encouraged and prayed for me along the way,
and to all who will read this book, I am deeply grateful. You are in my
prayers.

About the Author

Shannon (Kelly) Kurtz grew up in a large Irish-Catholic family in Bay City, Michigan, attending twelve years of parochial school. After two years of college, Shannon joined the United States Navy. She spent most of her four-year tour in the Norfolk, Virginia area, where she met her husband, Glenn Kurtz, a career naval officer. While they were stationed at the U.S. Naval Base at Guantánamo Bay, Cuba, Shannon had a deep spiritual re-conversion, which led her out of the Catholic Church into Evangelical Protestantism. She came Home to the Church in 2001, after twenty years away.

Shannon has a B.A. in History from New York Regent's University. She loved her years as a stay-at-home Mom, then worked in various positions including administrative assistant, associate reference librarian, and writing tutor. *Peony in Adoration, Reflections at the Feet of Jesus*, is her first book. She has also had articles published in *Family Chronicle* and *Immaculata* magazines, and her poetry has appeared in *St. Linus Review*. Shannon and her husband reside in northern Illinois and have two grown children.

If you would like to learn more about Shannon's return to the Catholic Church, the CD of her story, "My Journey Back to the Church," is available through Marytown Press, at 1(800) 743-1177, or e-mail mpress@marytown.com. To invite Shannon to speak to your parish or group, you may contact her at shannonsjourney@gmail.com.

Reflections

Reflections

Reflections

Reflections